Delivering
Customer Value

Management Master Series

William F. Christopher
Editor in Chief

Set 3: Customer Focus

Karl Albrecht
Delivering Customer Value: It's Everyone's Job

Robert King
Designing Products and Services That Customers Want

Wayne A. Little
Shared Expectations: Sustaining Customer Relationships

Gerald A. Michaelson
Building Bridges to Customers

Eberhard E. Scheuing
Creating Customers for Life

Ron Zemke
Service Recovery: Fixing Broken Customers

Delivering Customer Value

It's Everyone's Job

Karl Albrecht

PRODUCTIVITY PRESS
Portland, Oregon

Management Master Series
William F. Christopher, Editor in Chief
Copyright © 1995 by Productivity Press, Inc.

Productivity Press
P.O. Box 13390
Portland, OR 97213-0390
United States of America
Telephone: 503-235-0600
Telefax: 503-235-0909
E-mail: staff@ppress.com

Book design by William Stanton
Cover illustration by Paul Zwolak
Graphics and composition by Rohani Design, Edmonds, Washington
Printed and bound by Data Reproductions Corporation in the United
    States of America

Albrecht, Karl
        Delivering customer value : it's everyone's job / Karl Albrecht.
            p. cm. -- (Management master series)
        Includes bibliographical references and index.
        ISBN 1-56327-148-6 (hardcover)
        ISBN 1-56327-095-1 (paperback)
        1. Consumer satisfaction. 2. Customer services--Management.
    I. Title. II. Series.
    HF5415.5A4245   1995
    658.8' 12--dc20   95-12452
                                                           CIP

00 99 98 97 96 95 10 9 8 7 6 5 4 3 2

—CONTENTS—

PUBLISHER'S MESSAGE

The *Management Master Series* was designed to discover and disseminate to you the world's best concepts, principles, and current practices in excellent management. We present this information in a concise and easy-to-use format to provide you with the tools and techniques you need to stay abreast of this rapidly accelerating world of ideas.

World class competitiveness requires managers today to be thoroughly informed about how and what other internationally successful managers are doing. What works? What doesn't? and Why?

Management is often considered a "neglected art." It is not possible to know how to manage before you are made a manager. But once you become a manager you are expected to know how to manage and to do it well, right from the start.

One result of this neglect in management training has been managers who rely on control rather than creativity. Certainly, managers in this century have shown a distinct neglect of workers as creative human beings. The idea that employees are an organization's most valuable asset is still very new. How managers can inspire and direct the creativity and intelligence of everyone involved in the work of an organization has only begun to emerge.

Perhaps if we consider management as a "science" the task of learning how to manage well will be easier. A scientist begins with an hypothesis and then runs experiments to observe whether the hypothesis is correct. Scientists depend on detailed notes about the experiment—the timing, the ingredients, the amounts—and carefully record all results as they test new hypotheses. Certain things come to be known by this method; for instance, that water always consists of one part oxygen and two parts hydrogen.

We as managers must learn from our experience and from the experience of others. The scientific approach provides a model for learning. Science begins with vision and desired outcomes, and achieves its purpose through observation, experiment, and analysis of precisely recorded results. And then what is newly discovered is shared so that each person's research will build on the work of others.

Our organizations, however, rarely provide the time for learning or experimentation. As a manager, you need information from those who have already experimented and learned and recorded their results. You need it in brief, clear, and detailed form so that you can apply it immediately.

It is our purpose to help you confront the difficult task of managing in these turbulent times. As the shape of leadership changes, the *Management Master Series* will continue to bring you the best learning available to support your own increasing artistry in the evolving science of management.

We at Productivity Press are grateful to William F. Christopher and our staff of editors who have searched out those masters with the knowledge, experience, and ability to write concisely and completely on excellence in management practice. We wish also to thank the individual volume authors; Diane Asay, project manager; Julie Zinkus, manuscript editor; Karen Jones, managing editor; Lisa Hoberg and Mary Junewick, editorial support; Bill Stanton, design and production management; Susan Swanson, production coordination; Rohani Design, graphics, page design, and composition.

Norman Bodek
Publisher

1

IT'S THE CUSTOMER, STUPID!

WHY ALL THE TALK ABOUT CUSTOMER SATISFACTION?

Businesses all over the world are rediscovering the customer. Some have never lost sight of their customers, but a remarkable number of them have.

For years the management experts, business-school professors, and senior executives of large firms talked about markets, marketing, market share, competition, competitive strategy, products, capital, and profits. Curiously, the word "customer" has been very scarce in the management vocabulary for a long time.

As all of the developed countries have expanded into service economies, most of which now dwarf their manufacturing sectors, the new emphasis on *service management* is forcing all business leaders to turn back to the customer as the key to business success and even survival.

It's becoming increasingly obvious that the only thing that really matters in the new world of business is *delivering customer value*: doing things well in order to win and keep the customer's business.

WHAT IS CUSTOMER VALUE?

> *Customer value* is the ultimate benefit,
> as defined by the customer,
> of the product or service you provide.

Customer value is the basic truth of any business transaction; it is the litmus test of business success. Customer value is not your product or service itself nor is it a feature of your product or service. Rather it is the personal and individual *meaning* it has for the person experiencing it. It's not the gasoline, but what the gasoline does for the customer, that constitutes the value. It's not the surgery, but the restoration of health that the customer values. It's not the remodeled office, but the usefulness and enjoyment the customer gets from the premises.

The traditional distinction between products and services is becoming obsolete. Total customer value involves both tangible and intangible aspects. We have to manage them together. The customer value premise—the *perceived worth of an outcome*—is a helpful concept for fusing them together.

TALK IS CHEAP

Mark Twain said, "Everybody talks about the weather, but nobody does anything about it." And that's still the way it is with customer-centeredness in too many businesses: just talk. Hardly anybody denies that being customer-focused is a good thing. Who would claim that we should abuse, neglect, or antagonize our customers? Yet for many businesses, perhaps most, "customer focus" is still nothing more than a buzz-phrase, a slogan, or a "flavor of the month."

It's not enough just to talk about customer focus. Slogans aren't enough. Flowery phrases and big promises aren't enough. Customer focus means action, if it is ever to be anything more than just another business fad.

What things does your organization *actually do* to create real value for its customers and build a sustainable competitive advantage? What are the actual *practices* your people use to create customer value? What do your systems, methods, policies, and procedures contribute to customer value? How do your leaders make customer value happen throughout the organization?

These are very important questions, because:

Creating customer value is everyone's job.

EVERYBODY HAS A CUSTOMER

If you're not serving the customer,
your job is to serve somebody who is.

This is the principle of *internal service*. It means that everybody across the organization and everybody up and down the ladder has customers, from the front-line worker, who has contact with the external paying customer, all the way through the organization to the various support units—and in fact, all the way up to the chief executive.

No one can be exempt from the responsibility to create, or contribute to, the ultimate value for the customer. In this brief book we will explore the contributions required of all members of the organization in making it successful.

Front-Line Employees Have Customers

We all know that the actual, customer-facing employees must create value at the various "moments of truth" when they interact with external customers. But we also have to remember that those who work in the back room, unseen by the customers, still have customers of their own. Their customers are the other employees and units who depend on them to get their own individual jobs done.

Supervisors Have Customers

Even when a unit has regular or occasional contact with paying customers, the unit leader has to think about the internal customers of his or her unit, especially if he or she supervises an internal "support" group. In addition, the employees are actually customers of the supervisor, who has to perform the service of competently leading the unit to accomplish its mission.

Middle Managers Have Customers

Many middle managers do not deal directly with customers, but they still must be accountable for serving the needs of the organizational groups and units under their area of responsibility. They must be conscious of the value their groups create for the organization, so they can create value for the ultimate customer.

Executives Have Customers

To lead is to serve. The executive leaders of the organization must be accountable for their contributions to its success. This means they must create value for those who create value. Their customers are all of the other subordinate leaders, and ultimately, the employees whom those leaders serve.

The Chief Executive Has Customers

Even the chief executive, or more accurately, especially the chief executive, has customers. His or her job is to serve those who serve. By providing the vision, direction, philosophy, values, and priorities, and by acting out the key values for success, he or she must create value for all members of the organization, as well as indirectly for the ultimate customer.

TOTAL QUALITY AND CUSTOMER FOCUS

Because a total quality effort must focus on both internal customers and external customers, customer value must be the starting point for all quality improvement efforts. Why improve a process if it doesn't ultimately meet a need, solve a problem, or add value?

Too many quality programs are tool-and-technique oriented rather than customer-value oriented; process oriented rather than outcome oriented. Too many of them get bogged down in numbers exercises rather than focusing on the strategic needs of the organization.

When we get everybody in the organization to think in terms of contributing to the ultimate customer value, as well as serving the needs of his or her internal customers, then we can make it a truly successful customer-focused business.

2

CREATING VALUE

THE SERVICE TRIANGLE

The service triangle model, shown in Figure 1, helps you think about customer focus and customer value in terms of all of the participants involved: the customers, the employees, the leaders, and the organization itself. By putting the customer in the center of the diagram, we can interrelate the three critical success factors for creating customer value.

The Three Keys to Customer Value

- Customer-focused business strategy

- Customer-oriented employees

- Customer-friendly systems

The Customer

People who want quality programs to succeed are rapidly realizing that customer focus must be the keystone of any effort to improve the organization's way of doing things. Isolated quality programs that measure and

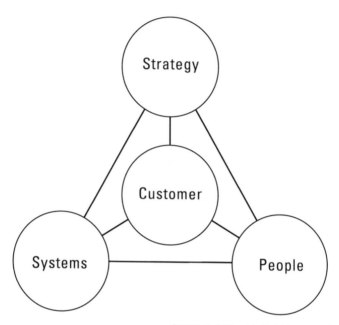

Figure 1. The Service Triangle

count things for the sake of measuring and counting are going out of style fast. This is why the *customer* goes at the center of the service triangle.

Strategy

People are also realizing that the basic demands of business strategy are what drive an organizationwide quality effort. What do we want to be, and how do we intend to do business? If the vision, mission, core values, and key competitive concept of the organization are not clear, a quality program will suffer from lack of focus and direction. This is why the element of *strategy* goes at the top of the service triangle.

People

A hard lesson of the traditional manufacturing style approach to quality is that the effort needs to have an element of *heart* if it is to succeed. Too many quality efforts begin as administrative, analytical, mechanistic, control-oriented, dehumanized, standards-based management attempts to tighten up the organization rather than loosen it up and empower the people to make their own individual quality commitments. This is why doctrinaire, mechanistic "systems" are ultimately doomed to failure. And this is why *people* are fundamental to, not an obstacle in, the service triangle.

Systems

The all-important *systems* go into the service triangle because they are the means for achieving the ends of superior customer value. All of the methods, procedures, equipment, machinery, tools, facilities, work processes, distribution systems, organizational structures, and information systems must work toward the ultimate purpose of creating or adding value—either for the external customers or for the internal customers who depend on support departments to achieve their missions.

Synergy of the Service Triangle

The most important idea the service triangle conveys is the *combination* of these three organizational priorities and their impact on the customer's experience and perception of value. Strategy drives and enlightens the entire approach to the business, and consequently, the organization's attitudes about what quality is and what it looks like to the customer. People need to understand the customer and the business strategy, because ultimately they are the ones who must make it a reality.

The design of the systems must also reflect the business strategy. How should we organize to create and deliver the kinds of value the customer seeks? We need customer-friendly systems in all areas of the operation, whether the customers are external or internal.

And, of course, the design of the systems must support the people who have to deliver value. They need information, resources, and methods—the ways and means for creating an outstanding customer experience.

And, finally, all three of these components of quality impinge upon the customer's experience and lead him or her to form an impression of the value we provide.

Use the service triangle as an effective communication tool in getting everyone in the organization to think in terms of *total customer value*, not just their own small part of it.

YOUR CUSTOMER VALUE PACKAGE

Every business has its own particular *customer value package*. It is the sum total of everything the business provides, both tangible and intangible, to its customers. We can systematically describe and analyze the customer value package in terms of seven key components:

1. Environment. The customer's environment is the physical setting in which the customer experiences the "delivery" of the "product," for example, the inside of a retail store, a hotel, a post office, a hospital, the cabin of an airplane, and the slopes of a ski resort.

2. Sensory experience. A sensory experience affects the perception of value, such as the flavor of food, the visual appeal of a retail environment, any experience of pain or discomfort, temperature, humidity, background music or sound level, and the mood or ambience of a facility.

3. Interpersonal dynamics. The customer interacts with those who deliver what he or she seeks. Examples of interpersonal dynamics are telephone conversations, face-to-face encounters with sales people, bodily contact such as in health care, and the demeanor of a person who delivers or repairs an item.

4. Deliverables. Anything the customer takes custody of, even temporarily, such as an item of merchandise, a tray of food on an airplane, bank statements and other documents, and medications is a deliverable.

5. Procedures. To function as a customer, a person has to follow procedures such as filling out forms, providing information, visiting various physical facilities, making payments, and waiting in lines.

6. Information. A person needs certain information to function as a customer, such as signs that tell which way to go, financial figures on a statement, instructions for installing or using a piece of equipment, pricing schedules, and knowing what to expect during and after a medical treatment.

7. Finances. The customer pays for the total experience and reacts to the nature of the financial interaction, for example, price or fee structures, billing methods, refunds or rebates, discount terms, guarantees, and collateral value such as volume bonuses.

Virtually every organization has these seven key components in its customer value package, including internal departments that serve organizational customers. Each of the seven elements contributes in some way to the customer's overall perception of value received. Each deserves careful analysis and continuous attention to identify opportunities for improvement.

The ultimate purpose of any quality improvement effort should be to maximize the appeal of the customer

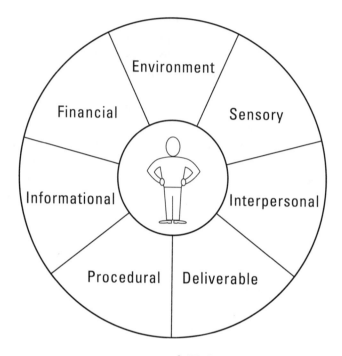

Figure 2. The Customer Value Package

value packages offered at all levels, to all customers, both external and internal, within the framework of a cost-effective way of doing business.

CYCLES OF VALUE

Now let's take the customer's point of view more directly, and inspect your service "product" from outside your business. Let's see how the customer actually experiences the value your organization supposedly delivers.

Let's look at the *cycle of value*, which is the series of personal experiences the customer goes through in doing business with you. A cycle of value, or simply "value cycle," is any repeatable sequence of events involving the customer that forms a complete service product. Every business has its particular set of value cycles, by means of which it manages—or fails to manage—the customer's experience.

As Figure 3 illustrates, a value cycle starts with a first experience, or moment of truth, followed by a series of various other moments of truth, and concluding with a final one at which the customer considers the cycle complete.

A typical value cycle might be something as simple as making a purchase in a department store, or as complex as flying from one country to another. There is a value cycle

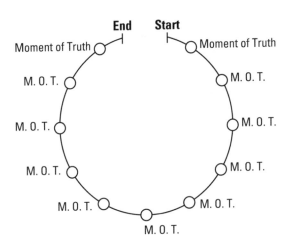

Figure 3. The Cycle of Value

for having a meal in a restaurant, one for going to a movie, one for having surgery, one for opening a bank account, one for renting a car, and so on. As customers, we go through a huge variety of these value cycles, trying to get our various needs met. As businesses, we must design these value cycles intelligently and manage them skillfully if we hope to win and keep the customer's business.

In many businesses, these value cycles cross over departmental lines and boundaries, abut all too often the people involved in them continue to think territorially. Outstanding service businesses tend to make their value cycles more "seamless" and require the various departments to work together to make things go smoothly for their customers.

No matter what kind of a value cycle it is, there are certain key facts to keep in mind that can help you make it successful:

- Total value, as perceived by the customer, is *cumulative;* it is the sum total of all the moments of truth that add up to his or her judgment by the time the cycle is done.

- Total value is a "weakest-link" experience; one disappointing or traumatic moment of truth can ruin the contributions of all the others that went before it.

- Some moments of truth are *value-negative* for the customer, or at least do not add value as he or she sees it. For example, waiting in line at the airline ticket counter is a necessary evil for most customers, not a value-adding experience. Many car-rental agencies now use a high-speed, expedited check-in process for returning the car, for this very reason. The customer's perception of value received and when he or she finishes using the car. The process of returning it and paying for it are usually not part of his or her definition of value.

- Skillful recovery from mishaps is critical; if one moment of truth goes horribly wrong for the customer, you had better be able to do something special to make up for it. The remaining moments of truth somehow have to take away the bad taste.

- The more moments of truth involved in any one value cycle, the less the likelihood everything will go well and the customer will be pleased.

- The more hand-offs between people, departments, and functions involved in any one value cycle, the less the likelihood everything will go well and the customer will be pleased.

- If the people who take part in the various moments of truth along the value cycle don't fully understand the overall cycle and their parts in it, it is very unlikely the customer's experience will turn out to be anything special. Everyone is just "doing my job" and no one is really able to add value.

- If the people involved in the value cycle don't have any cumulative knowledge of an individual customer's experience, which moves along from one to another, it will be very difficult for them to know how well they're performing. Except for the very angry or very happy customer, they'll simply be passing the customer along from one to another, with no sense of added value.

Another way to say everything just said is:

> If the cycle of value is not consciously managed, the customer's perception of value will tend toward mediocrity.

It's a new way of thinking to focus your business on managing these value cycles, rather than on managing the various departments. Seamless service, as discussed later in this book, can be one of the most appealing aspects of customer value, and one your competitors may find difficult to match.

Every employee in the organization should understand the value cycle or cycles that include his or her work. Every employee should understand how the customer experiences the value cycle, and how the customer defines the value involved. By teaching employees to actually plot out these value cycles on paper and explore their meanings to the customers, we can make all of them more effective in creating value throughout the total cycle.

3

KNOW YOUR CUSTOMER!

THE PLATINUM RULE

George Bernard Shaw didn't believe in the oft-quoted Golden Rule. He considered it misguided. He said:

> "Do not do unto others as you would have them do unto you; their tastes may not be the same."

There is actually a bit of useful wisdom in that comment, especially concerning the issue of creating competitive advantage through customer focus. The "customer revolution" supposedly has been in swing for over a decade, yet true, customer-focused business practices still seem to be in short supply. The widespread use of customer-interface designs and employee behavior ranging from customer-indifferent to outright customer-hostile testifies to the gap between the rhetoric and the reality. Customer abuse is still just about as prevalent in the developed economies as true customer care.

Customer Research

Although many of the bigger or more sophisticated organizations are making a serious effort to bring the basic truths of their customers' value models into the center of their operations, we can't yet say that most of our business organizations have successfully done so. Most management and marketing people still delude themselves into believing they know what customers want. Real discovery-based customer research is still in its infancy, with most firms bombarding their customers with homemade surveys rather than listening with open minds to discover the real sources of competitive advantage.

CASE IN POINT: HOSPITALS

Virtually all reputable customer research studies in the health care field, especially in hospitals, have disclosed three critical aspects of the patients' experience that influence their selection of a hospital. Yet probably fewer than 25 percent of hospitals regularly measure their patients' perceptions of these critical practices. Almost all of them have patient questionnaires that ask about the comfort of the room, the appeal of the food, and the friendliness of the staff. Yet none of those factors are really primary in the decision to use the hospital again in the future, or to refer others to it who may be making choices. All are outweighed by the big three.

What are the three critical practices? They are:

1. Demonstrate a sense of continuity, teamwork, and connectedness across hospital departments. This allows the patient to place his or her trust in the overall competence of the institution.

2. Make the patient a cooperating partner in his or her care. Empower the patient to be informed and make appropriate decisions and judgments across all phases of the treatment, rather than forcing him or her to act as a helpless inmate.

3. Respect the patient's personhood. Treat him or her as an adult participant in an experience in which, after all, he or she has the most at stake.

The evidence is clear that these three critical aspects of hospital practice are the strongest drivers of perceived competitive superiority of one hospital over another. Yet one patient study after another reveals that patients still widely perceive health care people negatively. They are seen as condescending and paternalistic, as more preoccupied with their own tasks than with the patient's psychic state, and as very disorganized when they have to collaborate in an institution-wide experience of seamless patient care.

These are the big opportunities for quality development in hospitals. Yet many hospital managers still dutifully collect and tabulate survey forms that have nothing to do with these critical indicators. They're victims of the Golden Rule: They ask the questions they want to ask, not the questions their customers want to answer.

CASE IN POINT: BANKS

Let's not just pick on hospitals. Many managers of banks still seem to believe that they can win new customers by offering them toasters or carving knives. Many banks still emphasize free checking accounts as attractions for their customers. I know of no study of consumer thinking in which people name bank-account charges as critical items on their list of worries or life concerns.

Guess where most banks get their new customers? From other banks, not from their own marketing efforts. The primary reason people change banks is because they get fed up with the bank they're doing business with. Many banks find that they're losing—actually driving away—their customers at about the same rate they're gaining new customers from their competitors.

CASE IN POINT: RETAIL

How about retailing? Listen to television commercials for all the major supermarkets and what do you discover? Gee whiz, they all have the lowest prices in town! Every one of them. Instead of learning what customers really value, they've reduced themselves to hawking commodity products on a price-appeal basis. Very few have even succeeded with the smile training programs, aimed at making employees more friendly.

From the Golden Rule to the Platinum Rule

Who knows how much advertising money has been spent on meaningless messages that do not connect to the real value models of the intended customers? How many misguided marketing campaigns have missed their mark because nobody really knew what the ultimate customer appeal really was? Golden-Rule thinking tends to be myopic and not very strategic.

So the Golden Rule is dead, a casualty of the paradigm shift toward customer value. What shall we take as a replacement for it? We'll call it the Platinum Rule, and it goes something like this:

The Platinum Rule

Do unto others as others

want to be done unto.

It should go without saying that the first step in putting the Platinum Rule into practice is to find out just how those others want to be done unto. Only then can you begin to realign the consciousness of the organization, as well as its systems and practices, to create the kind of customer value that can give you a sustainable competitive advantage.

So gold is out and platinum is in. That may be a sign of the times—a sign of the new frame of reference that centers on a combination of competitive strategic vision and true customer focus.

THE SEVEN SINS OF SERVICE

Although we don't always know everything that all of our individual customers value, we do know some of the things they don't want. Research into customer complaints and customer satisfaction has revealed seven of the most obvious and most common sins that businesses or their employees commit against their customers.

The Seven Sins of Service

1. Apathy

2. The brush-off

3. Coldness

4. Condescension

5. Robotism

6. The rule-book

7. The runaround

The seven sins are mostly self-explanatory. Apathy is a sin of the uncommitted, uncaring employee. The brush-off is trying to get rid of the customer instead of taking care of his or her special problem or need. Coldness is coldness. Condescension is treating the customer as if he or she were incompetent. Robotism is the "thank-you-have-a-nice-day" routine with no spontaneity or originality. The rule-book is refusing to be flexible or creative in special circumstances. The runaround is passing the buck, and the customer, from one department to another.

Is your business a sinful organization? Get some candid customer feedback and find out whether, or to what extent, the organization or its people are sinning against its customers.

THE CUSTOMER BILL OF RIGHTS

More and more businesses are committing themselves to specific promises to their customers, and doing whatever it takes to deliver on those promises. Think of it in terms of a basic "bill of rights" for the customer: practices any customer is entitled to expect from your organization and your people.

Every one of these basic rights can be very challenging for an organization to fulfill. Study each of them carefully. Educate the people in your organization so they understand and respect them. And then get to work developing the policies, procedures, methods, and attitudes needed to deliver.

THE STAIRWAY TO CUSTOMER VALUE

Historians report that the Greek philosopher Aristotle believed women had fewer teeth than men. The way he arrived at that conclusion was very simple: He just decided it must be so. And that's the way many executives today come to believe what they believe about their customers.

The Customer Bill of Rights

1. You have the right to receive a quality product or service.

2. You have the right to receive value for your money.

3. You have the right to be treated with courtesy, respect, and understanding.

4. You have the right to be treated as an individual.

5. You have the right to be told the truth.

6. You have the right to deal with someone who can solve your problem, with no buck-passing, brush-offs, or runarounds.

7. You have the right to an apology, quick action, and restitution if things are done wrong.

The longer you've been in business, the greater the probability you don't really understand what's going on in the minds of your customers. A certain arrogance of tenure blocks many organizational leaders from innocent-minded inquiry into their customers' attitudes.

Ignorance or misconceptions about the psyche of the customer can lead people down the wrong path in trying to implement quality improvements in any organization. Too many quality programs start by measuring and counting tangible work products and processes, without any evidence that the alleged improvement contributes to the ultimate success of the business.

Aristotle could have relieved his self-imposed ignorance by simply asking Mrs. Aristotle to open her mouth so he could count her teeth. Instead, he conjured up the "facts" in his own mind. This kind of "Aristotelian" thinking dominates a great deal of the design and delivery of products and services today. And it is reflected in a great number of misguided quality improvement efforts.

Hotels, restaurants, hospitals, cruise lines, and many other types of businesses throw quality surveys and questionnaires at their customers, basing their questions on Aristotelian criteria conjured up in the minds of the marketing people rather than developed through skilled customer research. Many businesses don't ask for customer feedback at all, to say nothing of having valid models of customer value.

It makes good sense to think of customer value as forming a hierarchy analogous to Abraham Maslow's famous hierarchy of needs. This hierarchy of customer value has four ascending levels, from lowest to highest:

1. Basic. These are the fundamental components of your customer value package required for you just to be in business. If you're a retail establishment, for example, you must have a location that's clean, properly furnished and fixtured, properly staffed, and properly stocked.

2. Expected. These are practices your customers consider "normal" for you and your competitors. If you're an airline company, they expect you to have competitive prices, convenient schedules, edible food, and reasonably civil customer-contact employees.

3. Desired. These are added-value features that customers know about and would like to have, but don't necessarily expect, because of the current level of performance of your competitors. This is the first level of possible differentiation and superiority over your competitors. If you're a hospital, it means consistently friendly and caring staff, accurate and honest information about the patient's condition, systems and procedures that engender trust and confidence, and cooperative interactions with family members and significant others related to the patient.

4. Unanticipated. These are added-value features that go well beyond the learned expectations and desires the customer brings to the experience of doing business with you. It may be unusually fast turnaround, an exceptionally confidence-inspiring guarantee, unusual expertise on the part of your employees, advanced merchandise features, or many other possibilities. These are "surprise" features that can set you apart from your competitors and win the loyalty of your customers—if, of course, they really do add significant value in the eyes of your customers.

Figure 4 illustrates the hierarchy of customer value as a stair-step progression.

Note that you must have mastered the first two levels of the hierarchy just to compete on an equal footing. This does not make your offering particularly attractive in the customer's mind. You must get beyond mere customer satisfaction and move to the *Desired* or *Unanticipated* levels of value in order to make a difference.

Bear in mind, however, that features at the *Desired* and *Unanticipated* levels do little good if other features at the *Basic* and *Expected* levels are poorly done. A hospital that offers all private rooms, gourmet food, and personal luxuries to its patients won't get far if the place is dirty, the staff is cold and indifferent, and the meals are late.

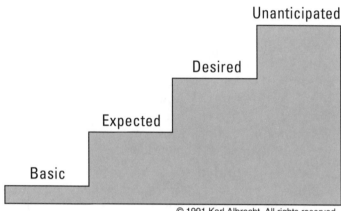

Figure 4. The Hierarchy of Customer Value

The hierarchy of customer value is progressive and cumulative—each level builds upon the levels below it.

Companies that offer superior customer value are those whose leaders have freed themselves from Aristotelian thinking, who have learned what their customers really value, and who constantly push their organizations to achieve that value.

4

EMPOWER PEOPLE TO DELIVER CUSTOMER VALUE!

USE ALL THE BRAIN POWER THAT'S AVAILABLE

The highest recorded human IQ score, if I recall correctly, was somewhere in the neighborhood of 200. At that level, the scoring system tends to fall apart, and the actual number means less than the phenomenon itself.

Organizations have IQs, do they not? Did you ever wonder what the highest organizational IQ might be? Indeed, what is organization IQ? How does an organization manifest its collective intelligence?

Some years ago, in a book titled *Brain Power*, I modestly drafted Albrecht's law of collective dumbness:

> Intelligent people, when assembled into an organization, can sometimes do dumb things collectively.

Surely we all wonder from time to time whether it's possible for an organization to stop making the same mistakes over and over, and to use the collective knowledge, know-how, and wisdom it has. Yet we still see collective dumbness demonstrated repeatedly in everyday organizational life.

Case in Point: A Hospital

I recently called a hospital in the state of Kansas to inquire about the status of a patient, who was the husband of one of my associates, supposedly there for an emergency hip surgery. The person who answered the telephone transferred me to another person, who consulted her computer and informed me that no such person was in the hospital. I asked her to double-check. She did and assured me they had no patient by that name. I was a bit confused, but had to assume I was mistaken about his whereabouts.

That evening, I was able to reach my associate at the home of some friends, and learned that her husband had been undergoing surgery in that hospital at the very moment I was being told he wasn't there. Is this a case of collective dumbness? And isn't it fairly typical of many organizations?

Use Your Collective Smarts

There's an even worse version of collective dumbness, much more profound and pernicious in its implications for organizational success or failure. It is the deliberate "dumbing down" of the work force through traditional management techniques that we have accepted and glorified for four or five decades.

While the Japanese are working hard at finding ways to leverage individual intelligence for collective good, many Western managers, academics, and management consultants are still working hard at figuring out how to exclude individual brain power from organizational processes. According to Dr. Evert Gummessen, a professor at Stockholm University, this is what Swedish managers refer to in America management methods as "the systematic stupification of the worker."

Think about your organization's collective intelligence. Let's suppose your organization or unit has 100 employees, and that each of them has approximately the average IQ score of 100 points. Multiplying 100 IQ points by 100 people, we get a total of 10,000 IQ points. The critical question is, how many of these IQ points is your organization actually using? Bear in mind that you've already paid for them, whether you use them or not.

When an employee shows up for work, you've already purchased his or her 100 or so IQ points, or at least you have an option on them. At the end of each day, you have either exercised the option or you've let it expire. That day will never come again, and the option on that day's IQ points is gone forever.

In a business environment where cost-cutting, downsizing, and process redesign are coming to the point of diminishing returns, yet profit margins are still being squeezed brutally, we must find new ways to make our organizations more effective and more competitive. Ultimately, even the most doctrinaire B-school thinker has to face the fact that the only remaining variable resource we can really exploit is the gray matter.

LET'S PUT QUALITY INTO WORK LIFE

The way your employees feel is, ultimately, the way your customers are going to feel. Not only the customer-facing people but those who work in all parts of the organization contribute to the collective spirit of service—or disservice—that customers experience. Organizations with disgruntled, angry, depressed, bored, uncommitted, or burned-out employees usually have disaffected and uncommitted customers to show for it.

A Model for Quality of Work Life

More and more organizations are beginning to include quality of work life, or *QWL*, as an essential element of their organizational performance measures. If we're going to put quality into work life, just as we put it into our products and services, we have to think about it in the same way. We have to define it, assess it, and continuously improve it. Let's start with a simple definition, then identify the critical parameters we have to assess and manage.

Quality of Work Life

The value to the employee of belonging to the organization, as he or she personally defines it.

Here is a fairly durable measurement formula for quality of work life.

Meaningful work. A job worth doing, a chance to do, create, or perform something that adds value to the world. Of course, not everybody gets to be an astronaut, a talk-show host, or a CEO. One usually has to start at the bottom and work up, but a person should be able to feel that the work they are doing is worth something.

Working conditions. Surroundings that are as safe, comfortable, and creature-supporting as circumstances allow. Not everyone can hope to work in a palatial office environment; somebody has to drill the oil wells and haul the rubbish. But the design of every job should at least accommodate the person doing it in a reasonable and humane way.

Working conditions also encompass the general political climate and the overall social and psychological atmosphere a person works in. One should feel free from intimidation, abuse, and duress, either from the boss or coworkers. For example, the emerging issue of workplace violence is becoming a critical aspect of this factor.

Pay and benefits. The total economic value derived from working should be fair-market compensation based on the value the job contributes and the amount of competition for it. If the job is properly compensated, but the person doing it is capable of earning more, the QWL issue is placement, not compensation.

Job security. Knowing that one will *have* a good job if he or she *does* a good job. Although this may not be fully under the control of management, nevertheless it is usually a critical factor in a person's assessment of the quality of his or her work life. In some cases, it translates into being told honestly and clearly what the possibilities are, rather than being kept in the dark about the future.

Competent supervision. A boss who knows how to lead, how to manage, and what needs to be done— one who knows how to treat people like human beings, who can communicate clearly and humanely, and who has the skills to lead a team to accomplish the mission.

Appreciation. Getting feedback from the boss and others that lets a person know that his or her contribution is recognized and valued.

Being involved and informed. Knowing what's going on and having a reasonable say in what's going on. It includes getting news and perspectives from their boss about important things happening in the organization, feeling they are part of a team, and knowing one's input will be heard and considered.

A chance to get ahead. Knowing that one has a shot at a job or role that is better, more rewarding, more enjoyable, and that pays better if one makes a good contribution in the current job—a true meritocracy where contribution counts.

Opportunities to learn and grow. Access to jobs, experiences, and educational programs that enable people to broaden and deepen their qualifications and job skills. A chance to acquire the skills needed for the next level while performing at the current level. This may also include growth opportunities of a purely personal nature.

Justice and fair play. Knowing that everybody gets an equal shot at the opportunities, that everybody lives by the same rules, and that people who violate the rules all get equivalent treatment. If there is discipline involved, it should be applied fairly, humanely, and evenhandedly. This factor also encompasses an overall atmosphere that is honest and ethical, and in which people are respected for what they contribute, not for their gender, ethnic status, or special standing within a political cartel.

Measuring Quality of Work Life

How do we measure the organization's performance in creating quality of work life? Much as we do for other aspects of business quality. We identify *best practices* and learn to associate those best practices with each of the ten outcome criteria just enumerated.

For example, with respect to the factor of justice and fair play, what are the critical practices which, if adhered to, lead people to conclude that a person in the organization can indeed get fair and equal treatment? Once we know those practices—and we already do—we can use the conventional questionnaire survey and supplement it with more intensive employee-sensing methods to draw a statistical profile of the organization's use of those practices. Then we can solve the problems around the gaps we discover.

We can't possibly tailor the organization to maximize quality of work life for everyone. But without some process of sensing employee perceptions of these critical factors, we have little hope of even knowing what our possibilities are for improvement.

A management team committed to quality uses QWL results in the same context in which they use all other quality results. It is all part of the self-knowledge that enables an organization to surpass itself. There is more and more support these days for the premise that an organization with a strong culture and solid employee support can go much further than one in which people are merely "human resources."

THE LEADER AS SERVANT

One of the Latin titles used to refer to the Pope is *servus servorum*, which means "the servant of servants." This point of view suggests that the role of anyone in a leadership job, whether it involves formal authority or not, is to lead by *enabling* others, not by trying to drive them.

In today's world, leaders are being called upon to provide a new kind of leadership: *servant leadership*. Gone are the days when a simple "command and control" style works. The old military style of the "kick in the rear" has outlived its time. It no longer fits contemporary social values, and it is no longer effective. People need and expect positive personal relationships with their leaders, relationships that help them focus their energies, work at their best, surpass their expectations of themselves, and feel a sense of satisfaction in what they have done.

Servant leadership is the capacity to lead with a service focus—service to those who benefit from the planned accomplishments, and service to those who work to achieve the objectives. It means working with a spirit and a set of values that emphasize worthwhile contributions. It means the leader sees his or her role as enabling or helping others to accomplish something worthy, not just being in charge.

The servant leader is willing to put empowerment above personal power; contribution above his or her own ego satisfaction; and the needs of the team above his or her own needs for credit and acclaim.

There is no higher religion than serving others.

Albert Schweitzer

5

NURTURE THE SERVICE CULTURE

PARADIGM 2000: THE CULTURE
AND VALUES OF QUALITY

The twenty-first century is now in sight. There are big changes in store for business organizations of all kinds. Organizational leaders at all levels will face new uncertainties, new questions, and new problems as never before. These may be the most exciting and interesting times we will ever live through, and they will certainly be the most challenging for managers.

As we move ever further into this new age of confusion and changing ground rules, organizations will be stressed as never before, and their structures and cultures will be questioned as never before.

We must ask whether the organizational cultures and values of the twentieth century can serve us effectively into the twenty-first century. We have come from a long tradition of industrial thinking, in which the managerial mind conceives of the organization as a factory, whether it manufactures anything or not. Our tradition is to make hospitals, banks, hotels, insurance companies, restaurants, and even government agencies look and operate like production lines. We have been trained to *objectify* virtually everything, that is, to think of and deal with the creation of subjective value by paying attention only to the concrete things and processes associated with it.

At the same time, this habitual Western mode of thinking conceives of the people who create the value as basically extensions of the machines and processes that turn out the "products." We have been conditioned to objectify them as well. So, we don't have people, we have "human resources." Instead of customers, we have "markets," "segments," and "niches."

Have you ever noticed the extent to which executives and managers in some industries go in renaming their customers to avoid having to deal with them as people and as individuals? To the gas and electric company you're not a customer, you're a "ratepayer." To the insurance company you're a "policyholder." To the taxi driver you're a "fare." And to the people in the hospital you're a "patient." We've spent the last five decades depersonalizing and dehumanizing our organizations, and now we may have to spend the next decade or two putting people back into the business.

Many management theorists, writers, and consultants, as well as leading executives are saying that the basic paradigm of Western management is failing, and that a new conceptualization must arise to support the much greater degree of complexity, diversity, and flexibility now required of organizations. As we move into an era in which leaders must help people focus on quality and customer value, the old mindset, or paradigm, of things and processes is being challenged by a mindset of people, culture, and leadership.

SIX BASIC DRIVING VALUES

What particular cultural forces have developed or emerged in the successful organizations that signal their ability to embrace this new "paradigm-2000" mindset? And, more importantly, how can we make it all work in practical business terms? Six basic driving values seem to come up repeatedly. These seem to be very strong cultural dynamics that are the hallmarks of customer-focused, quality-committed cultures.

1. Spirit of service. This is the general attitude and belief throughout the organization that serving others is an important, worthwhile, and honorable thing to do. It is a system of beliefs and values that people share and that their leaders demonstrate, reinforce, and appreciate. It is a personal, individual, and collective attitude that values caring, concern, and generosity toward others.

2. Shared fate. This is the sense that we are all in the same boat, and that our personal and individual success is inseparably intertwined with that of the organization and with our coworkers. Japanese companies are much praised for this spirit of group loyalty and cooperation, while some other cultures do not naturally seem to embrace it quite so fundamentally. Nevertheless the outstanding organizations typically succeed in building and nurturing it.

3. Codetermination. This is a pattern of solving problems in which employees contribute to and influence the thinking processes involved in significant change. Leaders and employees work together, think together, and search together for solutions to organizational problems that meet their common needs and interests. Together, they conceive of most major changes as codetermined rather than as the inventions of managers inflicted on employees. They see change management as a matter of cooperatively inducing change, not as forcing change on unwilling and uncommitted people.

4. Mutuality. This is the notion that if you're not serving the customer your job is to serve someone who is—the "internal customer" concept. In other words, everybody has a customer. The back-room departments who never come into contact with the paying customer are responsible for supporting the front line and other departments. Organizational leaders think of their operations in terms of contributions, not merely in terms of standard activities their people carry out. This attitude, when widely accepted and practiced, leads to a remarkable degree of internal cooperation and alignment between departments, and a widespread feeling of community spirit.

5. Empowerment. This frees frontline employees to make decisions and take actions that improve the effectiveness of their work and to add value for the customer and the organization. This includes providing them with the education, training, and information they need to operate with greater responsibility and autonomy. It also means providing them with the leadership that supports their growth and development, allows them to make mistakes and learn from them, and encourages them to take even greater responsibility.

6. Creative dissatisfaction. This collective attitude on the part of the leaders as well as the employees reflects the idea that we can always find a better way of doing something. This includes a certain restless impatience with standardization for its own sake, and a constant impulse to question current methods and practices. It involves constantly being open to new ways of creating or delivering value for the customer. Along with this we need to be alert to possibilities for innovation. Creative dissatisfaction is the driving idea behind the habit of continuous quality improvement. It is one of the things that fuels the organization's competitive momentum over the long term.

Figure 5 illustrates the six critical values of the service culture that revolve around the constant focus on creating value—value for the customers, value for the owners of the business, and value for its employees.

These six basic driving values offer an appealing focus for organizational leaders who want to align their operations around quality and customer value. Each of them is an indicator of the mental health and human vitality of the culture. Each arises from an effective way of operat-

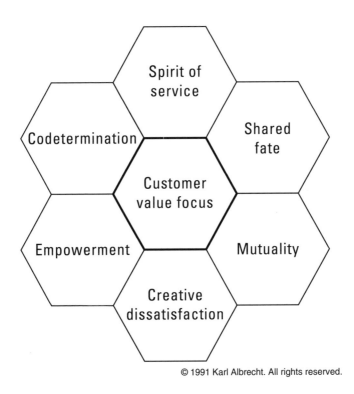

Figure 5. The Value Systems of Paradigm 2000

ing and a form of leadership that values human diversity, maintains a focus on business success through superior customer value, and supports the development of people as a basic part of its way of doing business.

6

DESIGN AND ALIGN
THE SERVICE SYSTEMS

CREATE SEAMLESS SERVICE SYSTEMS

One of the weakest aspects of organizational performance for most businesses is the "white space" on the organization chart. What happens *between* work units, departments, divisions, and operating sites can have a critical impact on customer perception, efficiency, productivity, and the cost of doing business. As the infrastructures for value creation in business organizations become ever more complex and diversified, coordination and cooperation—*seamlessness*—become more of a problem and more of an opportunity.

Free Yourself from the Process-Control Mentality

Yet we still don't have a workable management concept, precept, philosophy, or methodology for creating and maintaining seamlessness. The intellectual tradition of process-focused management, which we've carried over from the industrial age, falls short in this area because it evolved at a time when organizations produced rather than performed. There was far less white space to manage.

In the industrial era, all you had to do, basically, was define all the steps, tasks, or procedures involved in fabricating and assembling a physical product, then make sure the people and machines did what they were supposed to do. If the thing didn't turn out right, you had to track down the failing person or process and get him, her, or it back to the specified performance.

This approach works pretty well most of the time, unless the customer somehow becomes directly involved in the process. Then various unpredictable and uncontrollable factors begin to creep into the system. With the customer as a coperformer in the process, it is no longer possible to completely standardize all of the steps involved, although many organizations still try. Too many businesses still conceive of the customer as merely another process element—something to specify, standardize, and control.

The real opportunity lies in *practice diversity* and in *process orchestration*, not mere process control. Many organizations are struggling with this new way of thinking, and many still find it fundamentally contradictory to their long-accepted thinking processes.

CASE IN POINT: AIRLINES

Most major airlines are so absorbed with their own logistical problems that they have virtually abandoned all pretext of customer focus. Mired in destructive price wars, they've become so compulsively focused on cost control that they reduce their customer to the status of so many items of cargo.

Indeed, it is not unfair to say that most airline companies are really in the freight business, not the customer-value business, at least so far as their focus of attention is concerned. The "freight" happens to be alive, which creates certain problems. But despite the slogans about friendly service, standardization is still more important than individualization.

CASE IN POINT: HOSPITALS

Hospitals, again, provide a good example of this kind of conflicted process-control mentality. One part of the thinking process wants to see the customer, that is, the patient, as an individual human being, with personal feelings, wants, and needs. Another part wants to standardize and control everything the customer does: eating, sleeping, taking medications, undergoing procedures, and moving around.

That's why many hospitals look more like factories than places of caring and healing. Their managers can't let go of the industrial process-control mindset and move to a more diversified frame of reference that values managing outcomes rather than controlling behaviors. The result is white-space problems galore.

CASE IN POINT: GOVERNMENTAL AGENCIES

Lots of other businesses, and particularly government agencies, suffer from a "seamy" type of customer interface as well. And internally, as various departments deal with both internal and external customers, the lack of an outcome-based approach to performance causes people to focus on their processes at the expense of their results.

Bureaucracy becomes a way of life. Wasted motion, wasted time, and wasted money are all accepted as a prevailing level of mediocrity for internal convenience. And from the customer's point of view, the organization looks like a headless monster with no central brain or shared intelligence.

Service in a Diversified Organization

"Seaminess" becomes more and more a problem as you move up the scale of complexity and diversity in the way an organization creates value. Seaminess is lower in a "pure" production operation such as a soft-drink bottling plant, higher in a retailing operation that has a many-pointed customer interface, and much higher when the customer coperforms with an organization, as in the case of an airline, a hotel, or a hospital.

The high-diversity organization shows more variation in the way people and processes create value. There is more need for knowledge and social skills on the part of the people involved. As a result, a high-diversity organization creates value less by following procedures and more by putting knowledge and skills to good use.

If just following procedures is not the best way to create seamless quality and seamless service, then what is? In a general sense, at least, the answer lies in shared knowledge, shared commitment, and shared ownership of outcomes. With respect to customer outcomes, we have to help all people in the organization understand how the customer defines value in his or her experience. We must help them learn how to focus on the critical value factors as basic elements of the way they do their work. And we must help them think in terms of the total value-creation process, not just in terms of their localized part of it.

Managing the white space is a collective problem, not an individual one. No one person can be in charge of the seams. Making them invisible is an art practiced by people who know what causes them, and who know how to think, adapt, and communicate so effectively that they make the seams disappear. The job of leadership is to create the context, provide the shared vision and the common cause, and focus the attention on the creation of value.

TAME THE BUREAUCRACY

We're long overdue in curing the mindless bureaucracy of our business organizations. It's surprising, actually, how long we've tolerated the waste of time, money, and energy, as well as the slowness, confusion, and general mediocrity that infects almost all sizable organizations.

In an age when people focus on "six-sigma" statistical conformity in manufactured products, many tacitly ignore the much larger waste and ineffectiveness the organization itself generates. They may concentrate on shaving a fraction of a percent from the unit production cost, all the while wasting thousands of labor hours throughout the organization as people do things bureaucratically.

The new wave of interest in quality in government, for example, especially in America, will surely bring a much greater focus on the insane and unproductive things that go on in large organizations. We will need to develop the technique of *debureaucratizing* our organizations and making them operate much more intelligently. We have to change attitudes and cultures, as well as systems and procedures.

Think about any organization you've been part of, or closely involved with. It's relatively easy to point out policies, methods, systems, and work practices that make little or no sense, and that waste resources while adding very little value.

But reducing bureaucracy and keeping it down is often not as easy or simple as we would like to believe. Organizations have powerful tendencies to fall back to rigid, process-focused ways of doing things. Bureaucracy becomes like a cancer that must be attacked vigorously, systematically, and with determination.

The recent emphasis on reinventing the U.S. government has produced several amusing, but disconcerting illustrations of the Rasputin-like tenacity of bureaucratic systems. For example, it took the federal procurement office that coordinates business with firms that provide quality consulting services two years just to compile a list of eligible firms. They asked each of the firms to submit a huge documentation package, with many properly filled-out forms, pages of background data, resubmissions and corrections, and supplemental data. Our firm's submission filled several large boxes by the time we finished. The prospect of the government demonstrating its best bureaucratic style while procuring quality-management services offers a special irony.

Nevertheless, the job of debureaucratizing must be done. Organizational paralysis, waste, over-control, and inefficiency are too costly to ignore or tolerate. Almost all sizable organizations have opportunities to simplify and streamline processes, and put people back in charge.

7

FOCUS YOUR BUSINESS
STRATEGY ON CUSTOMER VALUE

WE NEED A NEW QUALITY MODEL

Now that the industrial model of Western management is undergoing major reconstruction, it's time for a new look at quality and a new model for excellence. We are all beginning to realize that the fundamental *paradigm shift* in management—worldwide—is bringing about an extroverted focus on customers in preference to the older introverted focus.

We are moving from organizations that merely produce toward organizations that perform—from structure to culture, from control to empowerment, from management to leadership, and from quality as a thing unto itself to customer value as a focus for competitive strength.

WHO'S GOT THE NEW MODEL?

What are the likely components of a new model for excellence in the new age and the new paradigm? How will we know it when we see it? I believe it should involve three things:

1. Combining objective value and subjective value, that is, a leap beyond mere physical product quality and a leap beyond mere customer service to a truly unified concept of value creation.

2. Focusing on the creation of *joint value*, that is, value for the customer, value for the organization, and value for the people who do the organization's work.

3. Building value-creation thinking into the innermost workings of the business strategy and business planning process, as well as into the organization's infrastructure and work processes.

We are moving into a time when both "quality programs" and "customer service programs" will become obsolete. Quality and customer service are abstractions and, ultimately, the attempt to improve abstractions is doomed to frustration.

In the new age and the new paradigm, the only thing that matters will be the creation of value. Process improvements can only be means to that end, not ends in themselves. Training programs for employees can only be means to that end. The same goes for technology improvements, organizational redesigns, and new process approaches such as self-directed teams and other trendy techniques. None of them will be legitimate unless they work within the wider frame of reference that enables the organization to create greater value.

Where can we find such a model working successfully, and how can we transport its critical truths into today's organizations? I believe we can find the answer by studying the best practices of the outstanding organizations in various industries and various socioeconomic settings around the world. I have spent much of the past ten years travelling to various countries, talking to the leaders of companies that their customers and competitors recognize as head and shoulders above the rest. From this research I have concluded that the best of the best have learned how to do certain critical things extremely well.

FIVE SECRETS OF THE QUALITY CHAMPIONS

Outstanding organizations all do five critical things extremely well. First, we'll look at them individually, and then we'll see how powerful they become when we put them together.

1. Market and customer research. Leading organizations understand their customers extremely well, not just demographically, but *psychographically*. They know the critical features in their *customer value package* necessary to win and keep the customers' business. They define what they do in terms of the customer's experience of value, not in terms of the characteristics of the products and services they deliver.

2. Strategy formulation. Leading organizations drive their entire approach to winning the customer's business from the truths they continually discover from customer research. They invite the customer to help them redesign the value creation process. They make no distinction between products and services, because they understand that all work is a form of service, regardless of whether it produces a physical thing or creates a fleeting experience.

3. Education, training, and communication. Leading organizations recognize that everything the leaders of the organization do communicates. They take great care to make the message connect with the vision, values, and business purpose of the organization. They believe in educating and developing people as a means of empowering them, and they understand the crucially important impact of shared meanings, shared values, and shared priorities. They understand what Professor Warren Bennis calls "the management of meaning."

4. Process improvement. Leading organizations continually work to improve, develop, evolve, and redesign the process infrastructure for value creation. They regard all organizational structures, systems, policies, procedures, information systems, and the like as merely temporarily successful solutions, constantly subject to reconsideration.

5. Assessment, measurement, and feedback. Leading organizations understand that information gives people power. They use measurement systems and customer feedback systems strategically. This is not to give managers a sense of being in control and sitting in judgment of the workers, but rather to enable the workers themselves to understand how well they are succeeding at their individual and collective missions of creating value.

TOTAL QUALITY SERVICE

Each of these five components is powerful in its own way, but the key is to put them together thoughtfully and skillfully. This is what the Total Quality Service® (TQS) model does, as shown in Figure 6. The TQS model is not so much an invention as a discovery. It is an attempt to describe how the best of the best live their lives.

Study the diagram to see how effectively these five components interrelate. Each of them individually, and

Figure 6. The Total Quality Service® (TQS) Model

all of them collectively, exert a powerful influence to keep moving the organization in the direction of customer-focused value creation.

- Customer research provides the strategic insights.

- Strategy formulation provides the critical meaning and direction for market success.

- Education and communication help everyone in the organization understand what it takes to win.

- Process improvement and feedback components are critical to an adaptive, self-correcting way of getting the work done.

TQS is not only a model for value-focused change management. It is also an all-embracing concept for doing business. Total Quality Service is a fusion of both quality thinking and customer-service thinking.

> Total Quality Service is a state of affairs in which an organization delivers superior value to its customers, its owners, and its employees.

Superior value is usually both tangible and intangible, objective and subjective. It is both externally directed, in order to win the customer, and internally directed, in order to benefit the organization and its people.

The art and science of Total Quality Service in the new age and the new paradigm will be to skillfully combine these five key components to make the organization successful. Those who fail to grasp the magnitude of the challenge or who fail to master the thinking process eventually will see their organizations become dinosaurs. Those who do understand are busy redefining the competitive rules of the game.

BIBLIOGRAPHY

Albrecht, Karl. *The Code of Quality Service*. San Diego: Albrecht Publishing Company, 1986 (employee booklet).

———. *At America's Service*. Homewood, Ill.: Dow Jones Irwin, 1988.

———. *Service Within: Solving the Middle Management Leadership Crisis*. Homewood, Ill.: Dow Jones Irwin, 1990.

———. *The Only Thing That Matters*. New York: HarperCollins, 1992.

———. *The Spirit of Service*. San Diego: Albrecht Publishing Company, 1993 (employee booklet).

———. *The Northbound Train*. New York: AMACOM, 1994.

Albrecht, Karl and Larry Bradford. *The Service Advantage*. Homewood, Ill.: Dow Jones Irwin, 1990.

Albrecht, Karl and Ron Zemke. *Service America! Doing Business in the New Economy*. Homewood, Ill.: Dow Jones Irwin, 1985.

Seven Dimensions. *Total Quality Service*, video series, San Diego: Albrecht Publishing Company, 1992.

Surveymaker: The Opinion Processor (software program). San Diego: Albrecht Publishing Company, 1994.

ABOUT THE AUTHOR

Karl Albrecht is a management consultant, speaker, and a prolific author. His 20 books on management, organizational effectiveness, and personal effectiveness include the bestsellers *Service America!*, *The Only Thing That Matters*, and *The Northbound Train*.

As chairman of Karl Albrecht International, he oversees the practical application of his concepts through a consulting firm (The TQS Group), a training firm (Albrecht Training & Development), and a publishing firm (Albrecht Publishing Company).

Karl Albrecht
Karl Albrecht International
4320 La Jolla Village Drive, Suite 310
San Diego, CA 92122
Phone: (619) 622-4884
Fax: (619) 622-4885

PRAISE FOR THE MANAGEMENT MASTER SERIES

"A rare information resource.... Each book is a gem; each set of six books a basic library.... Handy guides for success in the '90s and the new millennium."

Otis Wolkins
Vice President Quality Services/Marketing
Administration, GTE

"Productivity Press has provided a real service in its *Management Master Series*. These little books fill the huge gap between the 'bites' of oversimplified information found in most business magazines and the full-length books that no one has enough time to read. They have chosen very important topics in quality and found well-known authors who are willing to hold themselves within the 'one plane trip's worth' length limitation. Every serious manager should have a few of these in their reading backlog to help keep up with today's new management challenges."

C. Jackson Grayson, Jr.
Chairman, American Productivity & Quality Center

"The *Management Master Series* takes the Cliffs Notes approach to management ideas, with each monograph a tight 50 pages of remarkably meaty concepts that are defined, dissected, and contextualized for easy digestion."

Industry Week

"A concise overview of the critical success factors for today's leaders."

Quality Digest

"A wonderful collection of practical advice for managers."

Edgar R. Fiedler
Vice President and Economic Counsellor,
The Conference Board

"A great resource tool for business, government, and education."

Dr. Dennis J. Murray
President, Marist College

PRODUCTIVITY PRESS, Dept. BK, PO Box 13390, Portland, OR 97213-0390
Telephone: 1-800-394-6868   Fax: 1-800-394-6286

THE MANAGEMENT MASTER SERIES

The Management Master Series offers business managers leading-edge information on the best contemporary management practices. Written by respected authorities, each short "briefcase book" addresses a specific topic in a concise, to-the-point presentation, using both text and illustrations. These are ideal books for busy managers who want to get the whole message quickly.

Set 1. Great Management Ideas

Management Alert: Don't Reform—Transform!
Michael J. Kami
Transform your corporation: adapt faster, be more productive, perform better.

Vision, Mission, Total Quality: Leadership Tools for Turbulent Times
William F. Christopher
Build your vision and mission to achieve world class goals.

The Power of Strategic Partnering
Eberhard E. Scheuing
Take advantage of the strengths in your customer-supplier chain.

New Performance Measures
Brian H. Maskell
Measure service, quality, and flexibility with methods that address your customers' needs.

Motivating Superior Performance
Saul W. Gellerman
Use these key factors—non-monetary as well as monetary—to improve employee performance.

Doing and Rewarding: Inside a High-Performance Organization
Carl G. Thor
Design systems to reward superior performance and encourage productivity.

PRODUCTIVITY PRESS, Dept. BK, PO Box 13390, Portland, OR 97213-0390
Telephone: 1-800-394-6868   Fax: 1-800-394-6286

Set 2. Total Quality

The 16-Point Strategy for Productivity and Total Quality
William F. Christopher/Carl G. Thor
Essential points you need to know to improve the performance of your organization.

The TQM Paradigm: Key Ideas That Make It Work
Derm Barrett
Get a firm grasp of the world-changing ideas beyond the Total Quality movement.

Process Management: A Systems Approach to Total Quality
Eugene H. Melan
Learn how a business process orientation will clarify and streamline your organization's capabilities.

Practical Benchmarking for Mutual Improvement
Carl G. Thor
Discover a down-to-earth approach to benchmarking and building useful partnerships for quality.

Mistake-Proofing: Designing Errors Out
Richard B. Chase and Douglas M. Stewart
Learn how to eliminate errors and defects at the source with inexpensive *poka-yoke* devices and staff creativity.

Communicating, Training, and Developing for Quality Performance
Saul W. Gellerman
Gain quick expertise in communication and employee development basics.

PRODUCTIVITY PRESS, Dept. BK, PO Box 13390, Portland, OR 97213-0390
Telephone: 1-800-394-6868   Fax: 1-800-394-6286

Set 3. Customer Focus

Designing Products and Services That Customers Want
Robert King
Here are guidelines for designing customer-exciting products and services to meet the demands for continuous improvement and constant innovation to satisfy customers.

Creating Customers for Life
Eberhard E. Scheuing
Learn how to use quality function deployment to meet the demands for continuous improvement and constant innovation to satisfy customers.

Building Bridges to Customers
Gerald A. Michaelson
From the priceless value of a single customer to balancing priorities, Michaelson delivers a powerful guide for instituting a customer-based culture within any organization.

Delivering Customer Value: It's Everyone's Job
Karl Albrecht
This volume is dedicated to empowering people to deliver customer value and aligning a company's service systems.

Shared Expectations: Sustaining Customer Relationships
Wayne A. Little
How to create a process for sharing expectations and building lasting and profitable relationships with customers and suppliers that incorporates performance goals and measures.

Service Recovery: Fixing Broken Customers
Ron Zemke
Here are the guidelines for developing a customer-retaining service recovery system that can be a strategic asset in a company's total quality effort.

PRODUCTIVITY PRESS, Dept. BK, PO Box 13390, Portland, OR 97213-0390
Telephone: 1-800-394-6868   Fax: 1-800-394-6286

Set 4. Leadership (available November, 1995)

Leading the Way to Organization Renewal
Burt Nanus
How to build and steer a continually renewing and transforming organization by applying a vision to action strategy.

Checklist for Leaders
Gabriel Hevesi
Learn to focus day-to-day decisions and actions, leadership, communications, team building, planning, and efficiency.

Creating Leaders for Tomorrow
Karl Albrecht
How to mobilize all the intelligence of the organization to create value for customers.

Total Quality: A Framework for Leadership
D. Otis Wolkins
Consider the problems and opportunities in today's world of changing technology, global competition, and rising customer expectations in terms of the leadership role.

From Management to Leadership
Lawrence M. Miller
A visionary analysis of the qualities required of leaders in today's business: vision and values, enthusiasm for customers, teamwork, and problem-solving skills at all levels.

High Performance Leadership: Creating Value in a World of Change
Leonard R. Sayles
Examine the need for leadership involvement in work systems and operations technology to meet the increasing demands for short development cycles and technologically complex products and services.

PRODUCTIVITY PRESS, Dept. BK, PO Box 13390, Portland, OR 97213-0390
Telephone: 1-800-394-6868   Fax: 1-800-394-6286

ABOUT PRODUCTIVITY PRESS

Productivity Press exists to support the continuous improvement of American business and industry.

Since 1983, Productivity has published more than 100 books on the world's best manufacturing methods and management strategies. Many Productivity Press titles are direct source materials translated for the first time into English from industrial leaders around the world.

The impact of the Productivity publishing program on Western industry has been profound. Leading companies in virtually every industry sector use Productivity Press books for education and training. These books ride the cutting edge of today's business trends and include books on total quality management (TQM), corporate management, Just-In-Time manufacturing process improvements, total employee involvement (TEI), profit management, product design and development, total productive maintenance (TPM), and system dynamics.

To get a copy of the full-color catalog, call 800-394-6868 or fax 800-394-6286.

To view sample chapters and see the complete line of books, visit the Productivity Press online catalog on the Internet at *http://www.ppress.com/*

Productivity Press titles are distributed to the trade by National Book Network, 800-462-6420

TO ORDER: Write, phone, or fax Productivity Press, Dept. BK, P.O. Box 13390, Portland, OR 97213-0390, phone 800-394-6868, fax 800-394-6286. Send check or charge to your credit card (American Express, Visa, MasterCard accepted).

U.S. ORDERS: Add $5 shipping for first book, $2 each additional for UPS surface delivery. We offer attractive quantity discounts for bulk purchases of individual titles; call for more information.

ORDER BY E-MAIL: Order 24 hours a day from anywhere in the world. Use either address:
To order: *service@ppress.com*
To view online catalog on the Internet and/or to order:
  http://www.ppress.com/

INTERNATIONAL ORDERS: Write, phone, or fax for quote and indicate shipping method desired. For international callers, telephone number is 503-235-0600 and fax number is 503-235-0909. Prepayment in U.S. dollars must accompany your order (checks must be drawn on U.S. banks). When quote is returned with payment, your order will be shipped promptly by the method requested.

NOTE: Prices are in U.S. dollars and are subject to change without notice.

PRODUCTIVITY PRESS, Dept. BK, PO Box 13390, Portland, OR 97213-0390
Telephone: 1-800-394-6868   Fax: 1-800-394-6286